The Floating Stones of Egypt

THE FLOATING STONES OF EGYPT

OF

JAMES V. BARR

iUniverse, Inc.
Bloomington

The Floating Stones of Egypt

iUniverse books may be ordered through booksellers or by contacting:

iUniverse
1663 Liberty Drive
Bloomington, IN 47403
www.iuniverse.com
1-800-Authors (1-800-288-4677)

ISBN: 978-1-4502-8749-4 (sc)
ISBN: 978-1-4502-8748-7 (dj)
ISBN: 978-1-4502-8747-0 (ebk)

Library of Congress Control Number: 2011900573

Printed in the United States of America

iUniverse rev. date: 01/07/2011

DEDICATED TO MY PARENTS

ACKNOWLEDGMENTS

This book and its theory could not have been written without the effort and time put forth by friends and colleagues. A special thanks to Mr. Geoffrey Purcell for his researching and photographs that are used extensively in this endeavor, to Randy Hambly, Steve Ahern, and Mike Gaffey for their illustration, to Charlotte, Pam, Pat Nancy for editorial work and Dr. L. K. Bowser for his editorial work and for his work in submitting this to the publisher for print.

TABLE OF CONTENTS

Chapter I   The "AURA" of Egypt 1

Chapter II   The Dawn of Egypt 21

Chapter III   The Conveyance of Ancient Egypt 39

Chapter IV   The Stone Reminders 47

Chapter V   The Floating Stones 57

Chapter VI   The Canal and Lock Method of Pyramid Construction . . 61

Chapter VII   Archimedes 81

Chapter VIII   The Sumps 85

Chapter IX   The Stone Harvest 99

CHAPTER I

THE "AURA" OF EGYPT

The Egypt, Old Egypt, Ancient Egypt, Upper and Lower Egypt and the treasures of Egypt in all the pieces of literature written about Egypt there seems to be one common denominator or opinion expressed an immense admiration of the true Egyptian's ingenuity and accomplishment portrayed during the time of the Pharaohs.

There is not on facet of the ancient Egyptian life style that eludes respect and wonder. The pyramids, the massive canal systems, and the art works are just a few areas of endeavor that are synonymous with the "used" intelligence. There are many more, early surgery, astronomy unbelievable architecture. The list goes on and on.

Every time an exhibit, such as "King Tutankhamen's Treasure", is shown outside of Egypt, the admiration of the Ancient Egyptian era is shaped by more people of our present world. When viewing the treasure of the king a strange feeling of enjoyment surrounds its viewers. Thousands of people walked through the rooms filled with the golden art work. No loud noises can be heard. Just the sound of whispering voices praising the beautiful and varied examples of art and sculptures. At the very end of the tour was the exhibit of King Tutankhamen's death mask. Viewing it seemed anticlimactic. A strange aura of respect emitted by the mask was reflected in each viewer's eyes. This aura is felt when any wonder of Egypt is seen. It creates an air of mysticism, secrecy and respect, all at once. This feeling also spurs more and more research projects to explore Egypt's mysteries each year. It is unfortunate; however, that greed, avarice, and discontent have also been created. It is certain that more complete research could be accomplished in Egypt if some explorers and archaeologists had not plundered Egypt's ancient treasures for the past decades only for personal greed. Many artifacts created by the ancient Egyptians such as obelisks tomb treasures, and sculptures have been taken from Egypt without any compensation or gratitude shown. The British and the French were probably the worst abusers of Egyptian hospitality in the past century as evidenced whenever a person visits either countries museum of archaeological collections. These museums are filled to capacity with treasures plundered and smuggled from Egypt. A stark example of disregard for Egypt was when Napoleon of France used the Great Sphinx for cannon practice, thus obliterating the face of the Sphinx. I found this a sad situation when it came to light. This is prevalent with many monument of Egyptian histories. (Plate 1a & 1b) The Great Sphinx lower section still remains buried under vast amounts of sand in the lower 1700's.

The lion-like poses, the Sphinx guard the pyramid of Gizeh.

During the last research visit to Egypt to complete the photography of Egypt's oldest structures, such as the Pyramids of Gizeh, are slowly being reduced to piles of rubble. (Plate2)

Despite the efforts of several countries to help pre-serve the monuments of Egypt, there seems to be very little cooperation from the Egyptian government itself to help these countries. Many areas of Egypt that desperately need reconstruction or renovation are sealed off to out-siders for one reason or another. One example is closed because a dynamite factory is located nearby the pyramids. Another tragic example is the Great Pyramid of Gizeh. This massive stone structure is a stark reminder of what neglect and abuse affects such monuments. The pyramids outer layer of protective limestone was supposedly stripped off by the plundering Arabs soon after the decline of ancient Egypt. The ruin caused by time and neglect is noted when looking at various pyramids of Egypt. The interior blocks of stone, which are not as durable lime stone have begun to separate and decompose considerably, leaving mounds of rubble on each tier of the pyramids. Some efforts to protect the stones has been started, the work is quite slow. The mounds of rubble have made climbing the Great Pyramid quite difficult and dangerous. While completing the

Plate 1a.

Plate 1b.

Plate 2

photographs at Cairo for the pyramid chapter of this book, two people fell to their deaths when they attempted to climb the 400 hundred foot high structure. There are tourist police that patrol around the pyramid to stop visitors from climbing the pyramid, but the enforcement is poor. A slight money bribe to the police allows visitors to seemingly go un-noticed in their climbing endeavors. (Plates 3a, b, c, e, f, g, & 4a, b & 5 photos taken in December 1978) While discussing the decadence of the Great Pyramid, a short report on the condition of the boat resurrected in the 1950's from a boat pit near the Great Pyramid, should be dwelled upon. When the boat was discovered, it was assembled. A large shelter was constructed and the boat was reassembled and studied. . Being constructed of cedar, the boat is rapidly deteriorating in the harsh environment of Egypt. No funds seem to be available to hermetically seal the closed exhibit to the public. This is just prevent further ruin of this valu- able artifact of the past. Even though the boat shelter is quite large and could accommodate sightseeing tourists, it is closed to the public. This is just another example of the disregard for preservation of Egyptian antiquities.

At this point in time, something must be done. It is hoped that this book will help the world realize some of the problems that exist in protecting the legacies of Ancient Egypt. A certain amount of funds generated by this book's profits will be set aside for hopeful restoration of some of these legacies of Ancient Egypt. These goals are: 1. to portray Ancient Egypt as it was by using new theories and opinions. 2. to show Egypt as it is now to generate and procreate the "AURA" of Egypt.

Many of the photographs, drawings, and maps used to substantiate this book are entirely new, as are some of the deductions and writings theories that are expressed within. It is hoped that the book's purpose is understood as a meaningful project, and not as a vain. Endeavor. At the base of one of the pyramids of Gizeh stands a recently constructed building that houses the reconstructed boat. Pyramids made of clay brick and sand struggle to hold their distinct shape compared to the stone predecessors in the background.

Plate 3a

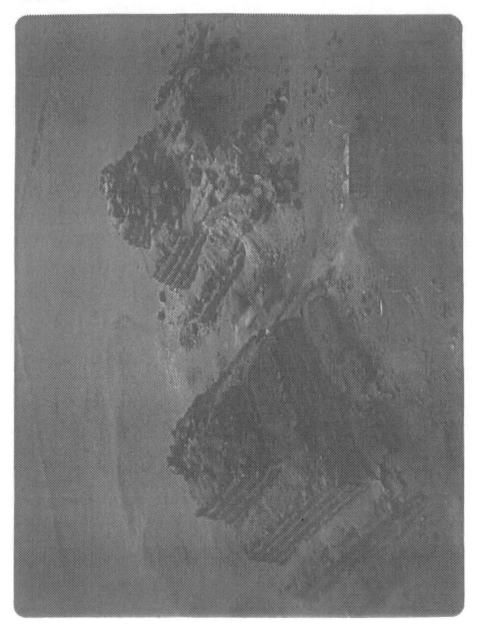

Plate 3b

plate 3c

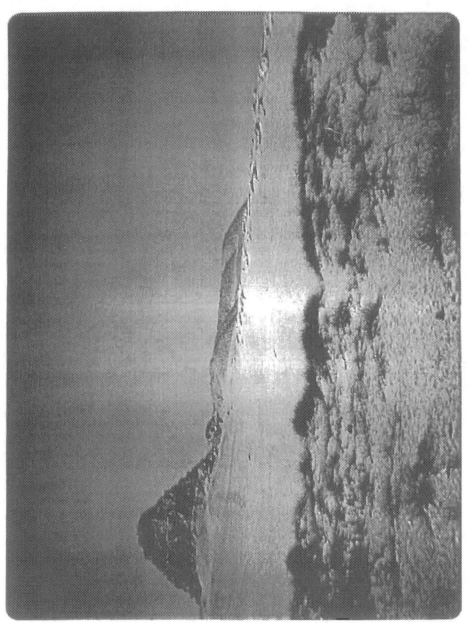

Plate 3d

Plate 3e

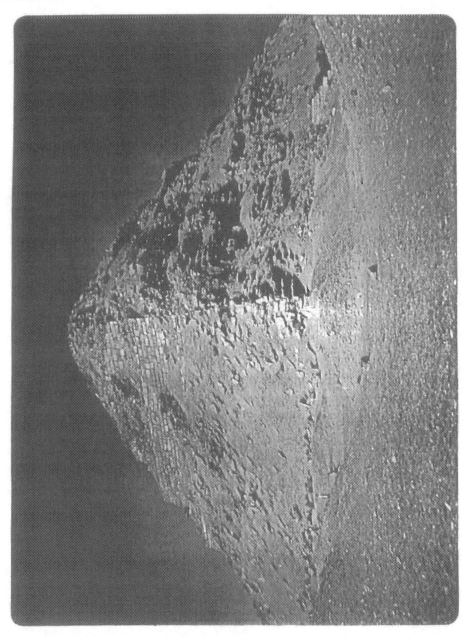

Plate 3 f

Plate 3 g

Plate 4a

Plate 4b

Plate 5 treacherous ledges create hazard to climbers.

Plate 6.

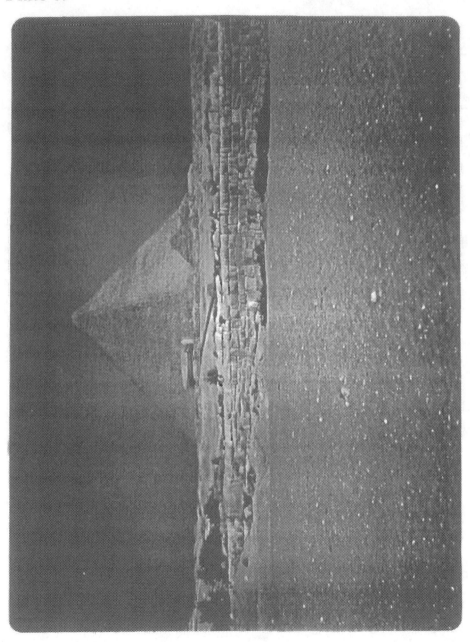

Plate 7

CHAPTER II

THE DAWN OF EGYPT

The fertile basins that spread for miles on each side of the Nile in Lower Egypt still supply bountiful crops. Silt left from the Nile flooding annually restores the land with fresh top soil. Most of the farming and cultivation techniques used are the same they were thousands of years ago. Water is still pumped by ancient waster wheels and the land is still tilled by oxen and wooden plows. By comparing Egypt's farming methods of today with hieroglyphs that predate the pyramids, little changes can be noticed.

The need for water to irrigate and supply the fields prompted Egypt to create a vast network of canals and reservoirs. Several canal networks that existed prior to 1000 B.C. and they are still in use today. The canals were so numerous that not all of them can be described or illustrated. For this reason only a select few will be described. One of the first people to visit Egypt and become aware of the canals was a Greek historian and traveler named Herodotus.

Between 465 and 450 B.C. he traveled about Egypt extensively. What he saw and herd was recorded in long letters and journals which he sent to his father who lived in Greece. Throughout his research of Egypt, Herodotus wrote vivid descriptions of the canals of Egypt. Some of the canals are described about in great length and detail, while others are only given slight mention. While studying the works of Herodotus, one must take into consideration that he was somewhat amateurish as an historian. He would exaggerate on some figures and facts that he reported. This statement is documented by comparing some of his calculations with modern day measurements and research.

In some cases the actual canal structures measured were not as large as he re- ported. This may be explained by the possibility that Herodotus was either inaccurate or that his writings and statistics were incorrectly translated. This should not cast a shadow of doubt on all of Herodotus efforts. Many of his descriptions of early Egypt are well documented and proven.

When describing Egypt's waterways, Herodotus first mentions canals when writing about the tyranny of King Sesostris (circa 1500 B.C.) of lower Egypt. The following transcript was in all probability related to Herodotus by Egyptian priests of Lake Moeris area in Lower Egypt.

"The King then returned to his own land and took vengeance upon his brother, after which he proceeded to make use of the multitudes whom he had brought with him from the conquered countries, partly to drag the huge masses of stone which were moved in the course of his reign to temple of Hephaestus partly to dig the numerous canals with which the whole of Egypt is intersected. By these forced labors the entire face of the country was changed, for whereas Egypt had formerly been a region suited both for horses and carriages, henceforth it became entirely unfit for either. Though a flat country throughout its extent, it is now unfit for either horse or carriage, being cut up by the canals, which are extremely numerous and run in all directions. The Kings objective was to supply Nile water to the inhabitants of the towns situated in the mid-country and not lying upon the river: for previously they had been obliged, after the subsidence of the floods, to drink a brackish water which the obtained from wells."

It would appear that, if so many canals were created, likely the main mode of travel during King Sesostris's rule must have been the boat. It is interesting to note Herodotus claims the entire face of the country was changed. The canal was now used for more than just irrigation.

In later writings, Herodotus gives a graphic account of King Necos efforts in canal constructions. "Psammetichus left a son called Necos, who succeeded him upon the throne. This prince was the first to attempt the construction of the canal to the Red Sea a work completed afterward by Darius the Persian the length of which is a four day journey and the width such as to admit of two triremes being rowed along it abreast. The water is derived from the Nile, which the canal leaves a little above the city of Bubastis, near Patumus, the Arabian town, being continued there until it joins the Red Sea. At first it is carried along the Arabian side of the Egyptian plain, as far as the chain of hills opposite Memphis, where the plain is bounded, and in which lie the great stone quarries, here it skits the base of the hills running in a direction from West to East, after which it turns and enters a narrow pass tending to the Southwest from this point until it enters the Red Sea. From the Northern Sea to that this is called the Southern inlet of Indian, the shortest and quickest passage, which is from Mount Casius the boundary between Egypt and Syria, to the Red Sea. It's a distance of exactly one hundred and fifteen miles. But the way by the canal is very much longer, on the account of the crookedness of its course. Plate 8 A. Early drawings by Norden show the lock system and water wheels were used to bring water up to higher different levels. A hundred and twenty thousand of the Egyptians were employed upon the work in the region of Necos, lost their lives in making the excavation._He at length desisted from his undertaking in consequence of an oracle which warned him "That he was laboring for the Barbarian". "Egyptians called the name of "Barbarian" all such as speak a language different from their own."

"Necos, when he gave up the construction of the canal, turned all his thoughts to war, and set to work to build a fleet of triremes, some intended for service in the Northern Sea, and some for navigation of the Indian Ocean." Plate 9: Point A of this early (circa 1800) map of Ancient Egypt shows the location of King Neco's Canal. Point to B makes mention of the labyrinths of Herodus. Point C reports that a Nilemeter was located at Memphis. Nilemeter's were used to measure the depth of the Nile before and after the flood seasons. Nile-meters were also used in both the upper and lower Egypt during the time pyramids were constructed. Plate 10 map drawn by F. Cope Whitehouse shows Lake Moeris basin and he course of the Nile River in 1880's.

The large canal of King Necos as one of the first Herodotus described recording measurements. Canal construction had emerged from its beginnings stages to become one of Egypt's early engineering marvels.

As canal designing and building progressed so did the ingenuity and engineering efforts used to build water locks and pumping stations. A geographic area that Herodotus devotes much praise to is the fertile basin of Lake Moeris. He concluded that Lake Moeris was man made and that what supplied it with water was an elaborate canal and lock system.

Lake Moeris and its canal system has been a controversial subject ever since modern day historians have researched it. Plate, 11&12 Aerial infrared photography outline agriculture areas along the Nile. The Black lines indicate water. Plate 12. The large body of water in black located in the left center of the photograph is the present day Lake Moeris. The large zone below the lake is a well-populated agricultural area. Trying to pinpoint the lake's exact location brings forth today some interesting questions and observations. And while attempting to find the original canal or canals that feed Lake Moeris, several conflicting opinions were discovered. The most important question that arose during the research was "Where was Lake Moeris's original location?"

Modern day atlases refer to the area known today by the name of Birket-Qurun as Lake Moeris. The name Birket means lake or sea in Arabic language. In an old atlas written by William Smith, there is a reference to the canal's that fed supposedly Lake Moeris. Plate 13a and 13 b. The wide expanse of the present day Lake Moeris looks like a mirage in the Egyptian desert. The boats seen in the lake is similar to the ones used in ancient Egypt. They have shallow drafts and are propelled with long shafted oars. Smith's reference places the lake southwest of Birket-Qurun. Maps drawn later by the cartographers of Nepoleon lend credence to Smith's evaluation of Lake Moeris. Herodotus described Lake Moeris in different manner. He said (loosely translated) that Moeris was fed by a canal that was monitored by a "lock system that required fifty talents of gold to open." A talent of gold was worth approximately $56.00 in American money at that time. Herodotus also wrote of a labyrinth of

Plate 8 a.

Plate 9.

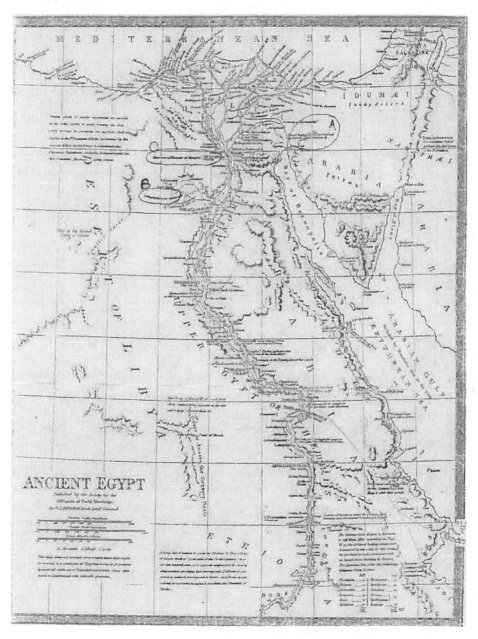

Plate 10

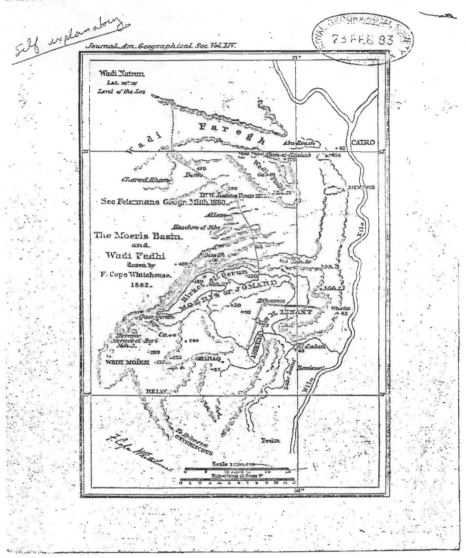

Plate 11

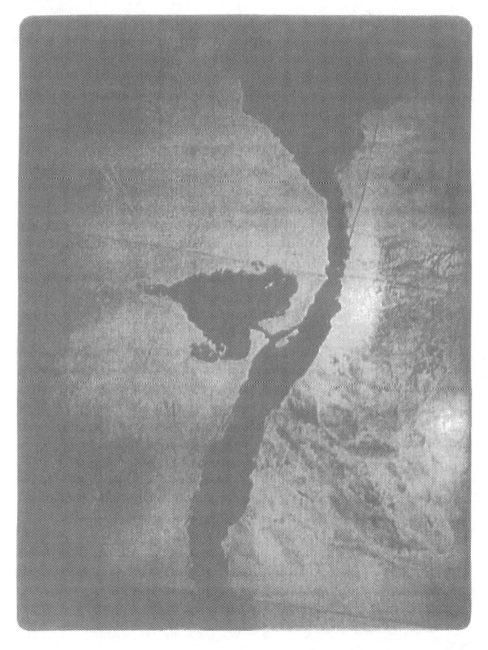

immense size and pyramids under construction in the "middle" of Lake Moreis, and on the top of the pyramids were statues. If this were true it could mean the Egyptians had possibly found a different use for a canal construction of buildings by raising water around the structure. This possibility could only be considered conjecture until the pyramids that Herodotus mentioned could be found. More research and opinions of later archeologists such as Petrie, Ball Caton, Thompson and Gardner tend to bear out a different interpretation of what Herodotus saw. Plate 14. Shows two pedestals that may have been "pyramids" Herodotus saw. Finders Petrie describes these rock structures as stands for large statues. The statues no longer exist to substantiate his opinion of the pedestals. There does appear to be many signs of any excavation to perhaps revel any manmade structures buried below the pedestals. The two stone pedestals are reportedly the ones that supported the statues Herodotus saw. This illustration was drawn by Limant DeBellefonds about 1870 A.D.(lower of this photograph). Unfortunately, time did not allow this area of research to be completed in order to help substantiate Herodotus's observation. The geographic locations of the pedestals do however; place them in the "middle" of Lake Moeris. Or rather in the middle of the plain that seems to separate "old" (the Plate original) and the present are known as Briket-Quarm (the new Lake Moeris). Plates 15 a,b,c, The pedestals that Bellefond illustrate in 1870 do not seem to have changed in the last century. Their size is well illustrated by comparing height of pedestals to people standing next to them. The size, weight, and placement of the stone blocks are similar to the Great Pyramids.

Indeed, Lake Moeris and its canal systems still clearly illustrate in another factor of ancient Egyptian persistence in utilizing the Nile to time the plains around it. After studying the vast canal network it is realized that ancient Egypt could not exist without the Nile, "The River of Life". Probably no other body of water has been studied or written about throughout time as the Nile has been. Early Egyptians in both Upper and Lower Egypt kept very accurate records as to almost every

Plate 12.

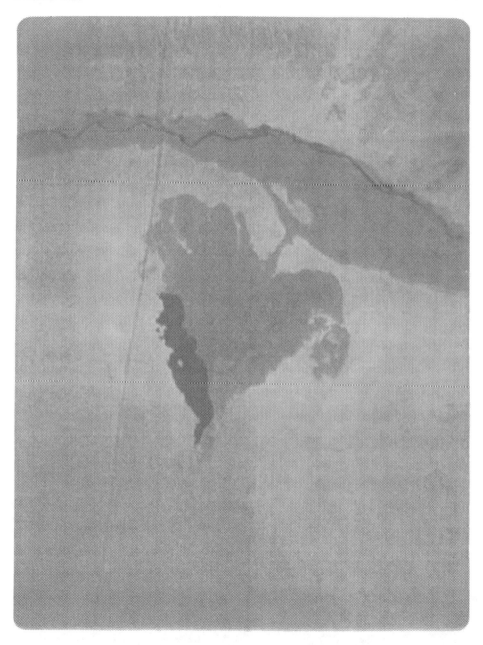

Plate 13a

Plate 13 b

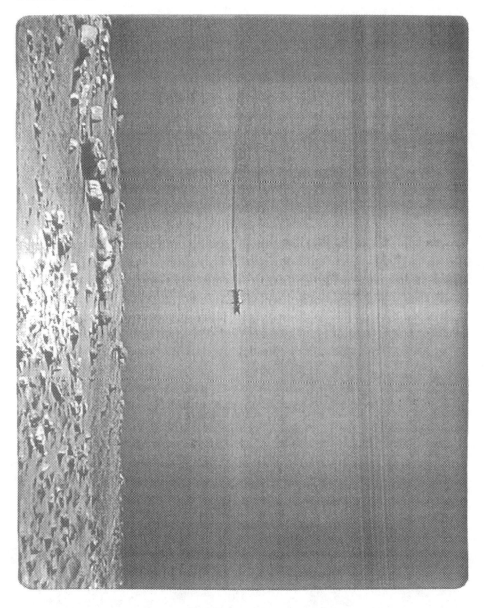

movement the Nile made. When it flooded its banks, when it subsided, how much water could be siphoned from it, the record keeping was endless. And no wonder, the Nile was and is Egypt's main source to allow existence. In later chapters of this book, the Nile's role in Egypt's lifestyle will be heavily stressed and how ancient Egyptian's utilization of the river could answer many questions that have been raise over the past centuries. As Herodotus stated, "The rising Nile has no bounds", it could be said too, that the Egyptians use of the Nile also knew no bounds.

Plate 14

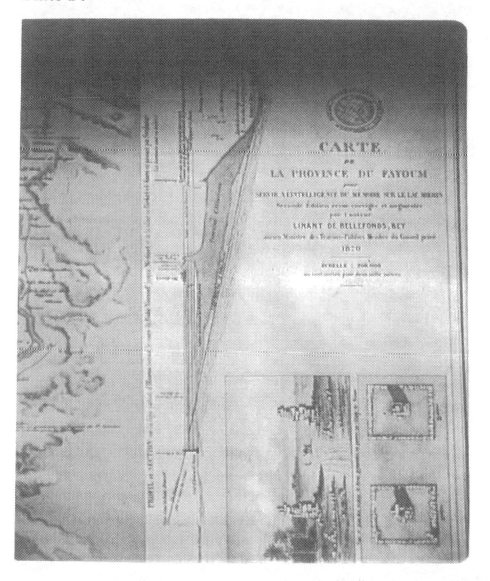

Plate 15 a,

Plat15 b,

Plate 15 c,

CHAPTER III

THE CONVEYANCE OF ANCIENT EGYPT

Egypt's picture writing named Hieroglyphs give present day cultures a colorful look into Egypt's past. They depict large oxen, camels, and various beasts of burden that were used for land travel. They also show the different styles of boats and barges used to travel the vast canal networks and the Nile itself. It is unfortunate that the hieroglyphs do not show proper scale in many instances. Often the boats drawn are vastly out of proportion to the cargo (human or otherwise that they transported and to the surrounding scenes that back drop the water craft. Although there is very little information written during the time of the ancient Egypt to show the accurate size and capacities of their boats and barges, there is some information available from later written observations.

Some of the craft described were merely constructed of reeds and were used to carry one to five passengers and limited cargo. These rather flimsy craft had a short life spans and due to the rather inexpensive materials utilized in their construction, they were probably used by the working or farming class of Egypt. The reed boats are still used today throughout Egypt and Sudan. See Illustration 1. The reeds of the Nile were bound lightly to create small water crafts.

The large boats were constructed of wood, tar and ropes. They varied in shape and size considerably. One barge, reported to be used by King Necos, was about two hundred feet in length. No other description of what material the barge was constructed of or how it was shaped could be found. But if the length reported was accurate, King Nevos conveyance must have been an impressive sight and a tribute to the boat designers of around 600B.C.

Earlier wood boats (circa 2000 B.C.) were unique in design as they could be disassembled and then reassembled by written instructions. The boat that was reassembled from a large Mastaba near the Great Pyramid of Gizeh bears out the aforementioned statement. In the late1950's the boat was removed from a pit that had kept the reassembled craft in remarkably good condition after centuries of non-use. The boat pit was airtight, and like many Egyptian enclosures, once it was opened its contents began to deteriorate slowly. The boat and the hundreds of feet of rope found with it have begun to meet this fate. As mentioned in an earlier chapter, some effort to prevent the loss of this craft has been accomplished. The boat is now completely assembled by following the instructions found in the boat pit. A shell-like structure has been constructed around the boat to protect it somewhat from the harsh environment of Egypt. This is merely a stop-gap measure as dehumidifiers are needed with the building to keep the boat from deteriorating any further. Illustration 2. This is an accurate drawing of ancient Egyptian cargo boat. Other crafts await reconstruction in Egypt, but perhaps, it would be wise to leave then in their ancient protectorates until suitable facilities can be constructed to preserve their antiquity. After observing older photographs (no new ones can be taken) of the resurrected boat, it appears that the craft was designed for ceremonial use, rather than for cargo carrying, as the draft of the boat is quite shallow. The oars of the boat seem to be designed more for steering the craft, rather than for propulsion, because they are quite narrow of blade and long oar shafts are attached to a framework above the deck at an angle that does not allow much leverage to be exerted to the base of the oars. The house (or cabin) at the back of the boat appear to shelter only a portion of the deck. If this was a designed for cargo use, the shelter should have covered the majority of the exposed deck. It is interesting to note that the configuration of this boat is not seen in any hieroglyphs found in Gizeh. Why? An answer could only be speculation. Perhaps it was not a common design or possibly, only a few were made. Because the boat is an accurate example of skills and materials used to build it in ancient Egypt, it is illustration 3, as a cargo boat, but as stated before it is not a reconstructed boats true use.

Illustration 1

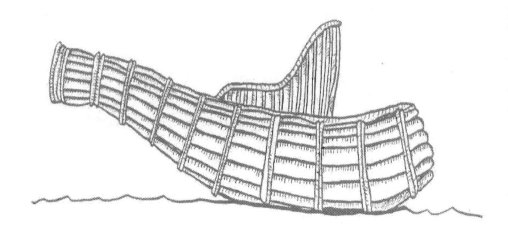

Illustration 2,

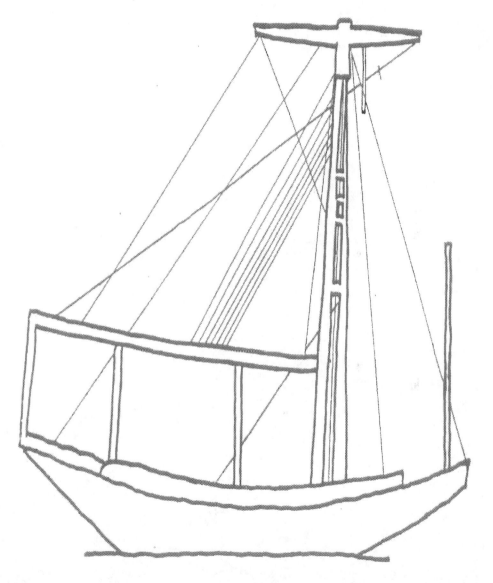

Illustration 3

Plate 16. A recently excavated boat pit can be compared in size to the surrounding structures.
Plate 16.

Plate 17a, Aerial view excavated pit of Gizeh.

CHAPTER IV

THE STONE REMINDERS

Of the Seven Wonders of the World, the pyramids of Egypt are probably the most famous and researched.

Without being too repetitious, as most books on Egypt echo the same comments on pyramids over and over, only a slight history is presented concerning the structures and then a new area of research will be offered.

The pyramids that dot the plains of Lower Egypt were constructed of different materials and designs. Most of the early pyramids were built of clay bricks and sand. Not many of them exist today as the materials used did not stand up to the rigors of time and weather. Some would be hardly recognizable as pyramids, but more similar to mounds of rubble and sand. The later pyramids were constructed (after 300B.C.) of granite, limestone and various other types of stone materials. Stone, being a more durable material than clay, slowed the decomposition problem that occurred in earlier efforts. As the building materials were improved, so were the designs used to build the pyramids. The later structures were made with more precision than their predecessors. Their height and overall size is more that tripled and inside them are elaborate chamber that were built.

More has been written about the Great Pyramid of Gizeh (also known as the Pyramid of Cheops of Khufre) than any of the other stone or clay brick structures. This is due to the high degree of workmanship and engineering that is evident when the Great Pyramid is studied. Its original height was over 470 feet and its triangular massiveness covers thirteen square acres. More than an estimated two million stone blocks were used to construct the Great Pyramid. The average weight of these blocks is about two and one half tons a piece, and some weight in excess of seventy tons. The actual weight of the outer layer stones (made of white tura limestone) is not known as this particular layer does not exist any longer on the pyramid. It is thought to have been stripped off by plundering Arabs soon after the fall of ancient Egypt. If the white outer layer of the Great Pyramid were intact today, the decomposition of the internal stones now exposed would be considerably less. One could only imagine how beautiful and stately the structure would be today if the outer layer were still intact. Still in the morning sun, the Great Pyramid takes on a beautiful goldish hue. In the afternoon the pyramid is grayish in color, and in the evening it takes on a brilliant red color.

Many of the other pyramids take on different colors as the sun rises and sets. The Red Pyramid of Dashir has a grayish caste to it in the morning and then turns to a brilliant red in the afternoon. Its name is derived from the afternoon color it reflects and the material from which it was made of in this case a redish granite. The Pyramid of Meidum appear golden in the morning, and then grayish white in the evening.

The many ideas and theories of how the pyramids were built are as different and changeable as the colors of the structures. The most common theory presented in books about Egypt is the "Ramp" theory. Perhaps why the ramp theory is most popular is that it is the easiest to understand. It merely states that a large ramp was constructed from the sand and bricks alongside of the pyramid being built. With the use of ropes, sleds and a vast amount of power, the large stones were dragged up the ramp and fitted into place. After the pyramid (stone or brick) was completed, the ramp was disassembled slowly to allow the builders to polish or decorate the outside layers of the pyramids working from the top downward.

Plates 17 A green carpet of date palms and contrast with the desert of Cairo. The pyramids in the background are miles from where this photograph was taken, they resemble triangular shaped mountains of stone. The "ramp theory" is somewhat supported by the fact that a few

Plate 17.

Plate 18, Modern day buildings are dwarfed by an ancient "step" pyramid.

hieroglyphs depict workers dragging stone statues on sleds while other worker threw water ahead of the sleds to cut down on friction. These hieroglyphs do not however show pyramids under construction.

The levitation theory of pyramid building is even less substantiated by known facts. This theory was brought to light in the late 1950's and it is a little more complicated than the ramp theory as it involves anti-magnetic and supposed visitors from outer space. If there is any fact behind the levitation theory, it must have been some sight, seeing huge granite stones float in the air from the quarries to the pyramids. If this theory is to be taken seriously, a person would have to use a tremendous amount of imagination. A fair level of supposition has to be used when studying ancient Egypt, but science fiction should be excluded.

Plates 19 a, 19 b. Like stone chameleons, the pyramids of Gizeh change color during the day.

Plate 20. The pyramid of Meidum stands out starkly with a whitish cast when seen at a distance. The old phrase "seeing is believing" is well represented by the pyramids. If the pyramids did not exist today, except only in drawings, it would be hard to believe they ever existed, but would be considered figments of some artist's imagination. Yet, they do stand as mute reminders of a vastly intelligent civilization.

Plate 19 a.

Plate 19 b.

Illustration 4 is in support of the ramp theory.

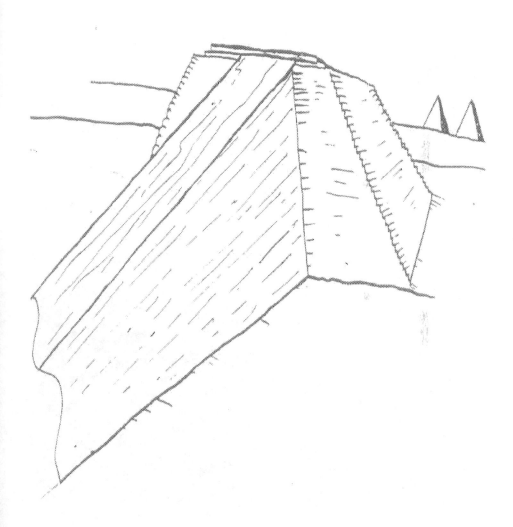

Plate 20.

CHAPTER V

THE FLOATING STONES

The ramp theory and the levitation theory previously discussed brought forth some interesting questions. What happened to the huge ramps that were built? Is it possible that the large stones used in pyramid construction "float" after more than six years of comparative analysis of some thirty or more large pyramids, the answer may be at hand? Using very little supposition and existing facts, it can be said that the ancient Egyptians possessed the following ability and skills needed to construct a pyramid.

1. Canals with lock systems.
2. Large boats and rafts.
3. Hardened tools for quarrying stone.
4. Crude efficient measuring devices (i.e. plumb Bobs, non-lensed sighting devices)
5. A seemingly unlimited manpower.
6. The intelligence and foresight to learn from previous design errors and evidenced by earlier brick to structures of stone. Comparing the earlier brick structures of stone.
7. Strict systems of government that would coordinate ancient Egypt and its people for better than 3000 years. (a feat non-comparable in modern ages).

Everything aforementioned tempered with respect for the Intelligence of ancient Egypt has been used to produce a new theory on how the stone pyramids of Egypt were constructed. The theory is named "THE CANAL

AND LOCK METHOD OF PYRAMID CONSTRUCTION".
Without recounting the hours of research and the amount of dollars
expended to present this new theory, it is hoped the following pages will
speak for themselves in an understandable manner.

CHAPTER VI

THE CANAL AND LOCK
METHOD OF PYRAMID
CONSTRUCTION

S tarting with illustration (5), the Great Pyramid (used as prime example throughout the theory explanation) is shown at a 30 percent level of completion in the middle of the square wall reservoir. At Point (A) is a stone filled barge making its way to the upper entrance of the reservoir. Point (B) shows the exit lock at the end of the causeway in the closed position. Illustration (6) shows the lock at its lowered position and Point (A) is a release lock to allow the in captured water to flow back to the Nile through the causeway Point (B).

After the disembarkment of the building material the lock was then filled and the barge raised back, with the use of ropes and manpower, to the lock entrance. More than one barge at a time could have entered the lock opening but, only one is depicted.

After the empty barges were pulled from the canal they were disassembled and placed on a "recovery barge". The recovery barge was then pulled back up the Nile to the quarry location. Plate 21 Water hydraulics was used quite extensively in Egypt. This drawing by the French archeologist Norden (circa 1790) clearly shows water being brought up from great depths to a large reservoir.

The massive blocks used in the construction of the Great Pyramid fit together so closely that a shim of paper cannot be inserted into the joints. The reason for this that the stone blocks are fitted together exactly in the same order as they were cut from their respective quarries.

The blocks were not lifted into position but merely slid into their prepared stations. Keeping in mind that no mortar was used to hold the blocks in place, odd angles of cutting combined with the stone's sheer dead weight had to be utilized to allow the structure to remain stable. Mortar would dissipate under water and yet a form of mortar was used. It was made of petroleum base and was applied to the blocks to accommodate easier positioning. Plate 22 Norden used the term canal many times when describing pyramids. Section b, of this shows the angular placement of stone inside the pyramid. Remnants of this grease-like mixture that was used are still present today.

Illustration5

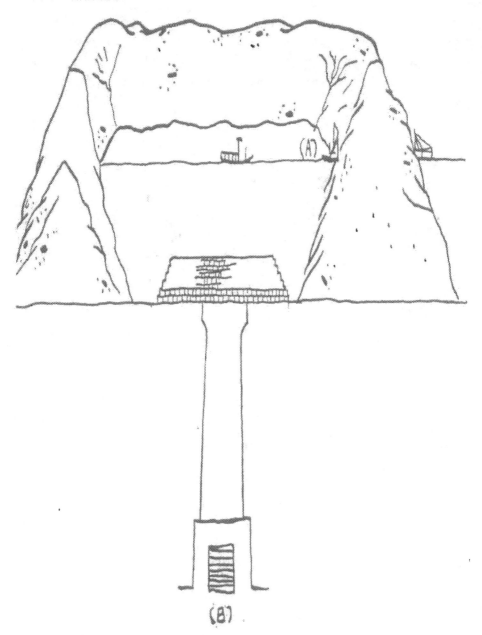

Illustration (6)

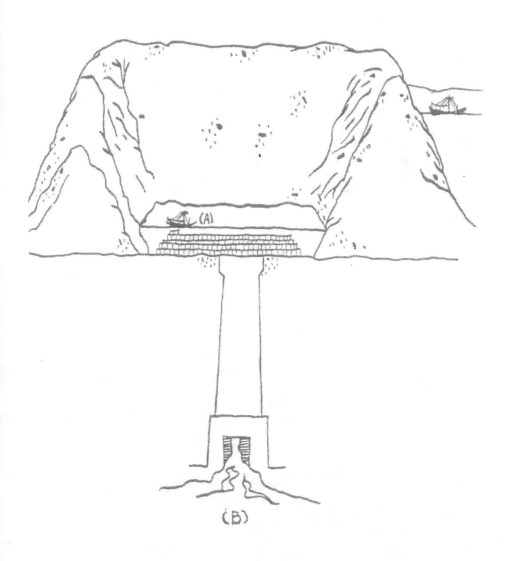

Plate 21.

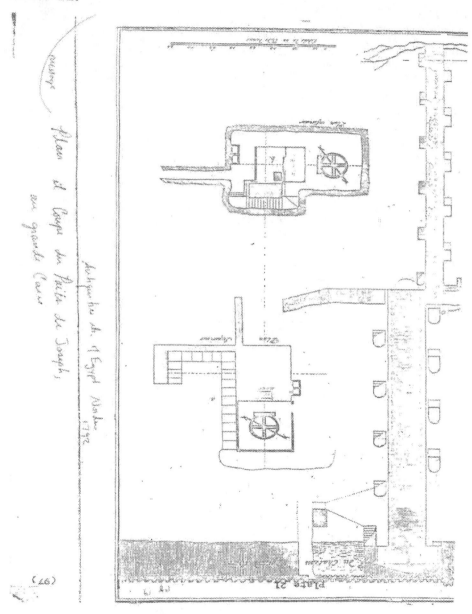

To further ease the task of positioning the stones that the pyramid was built of angles that protrude upward to the center of the structure. These angles are slight, but never the less are measurable. Plate 23. What is left of the foundation casement stones of the Great Pyramid clearly shows s degree of masonry skill. Blocks were laid into place in the same order they were quarried. Graffiti on the blocks is recent, detracting from the works of stone cutters. Plate 24. A tribute to stone cutting skills, excavation, and transportation of the finished product is exemplified unmoved obelisk. Hewn out surround quarry, weighing tens of tons, massive piece of stone would have been transferred by boat and placed upright at its final resting place.

The internal stone passageways were constructed to angular proportions. This is depicted by illustration 6, point B Grand Gallery. Also at point C are smaller passageways that also follow angular patterns.

Plate 22

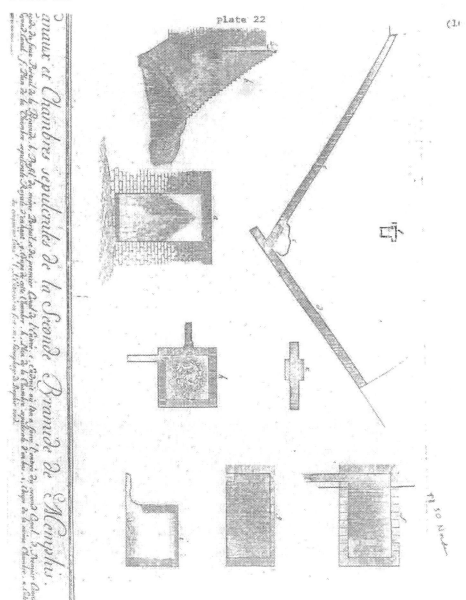

There is one chamber that was not constructed on an angle (point D Queens Chamber and Entrance Hall). This portion of the pyramid was never completed as it was an error in design. Level passageway could not drain water fast enough, therefore the Queens level aisle way and Chamber were sealed and the next step of fabrication was built utilizing steeper slants. It is interesting to note that salt like deposits are found on the walls of the Queen's passageway and Chamber created by long period of submersion. These deposits do not exist on the other passageways as they were polished and cleaned during the final stages of completion.

Above the internal structures but leading to them are the air vents Point E. The air vents are also at angles and their outside openings are above any of the internal structures. The reason given is that these holes were used to transport food, water and fresh air to the workers. It would, engineering wise be much easier to place the air holes on a level plane but the surrounding water would have defeated their purpose.

Plate 23

Plate 24

At the top end of the King's Chamber is the Tomb of Cheops and within it is the sarcophagus Point F. It is generally believed that the stone casket sarcophagus was brought up to the Grand Gallery and placed in the tomb. Generally is believed that the stone casket sarcophagus was brought up to the Grand Gallery and placed in the tomb. The casket is approximately one inch larger than the inside measurements of the entrance to the tomb. Thus, the casket was likely to have been placed on the tomb floor during the mid-phase of construction and the tomb built around and above it.

The top of the King's tomb is sealed by large cap stones Point G. These stone blocks were laid into place one on top of each other, with spacer blocks situated between them. This feat would seem quite impossible if not for the fact that the weight of these blocks and others used in construction is greatly reduced under water by Archimedes principle of bouncy (i.e. when one cubic foot of lead weighing 700 pounds is submerged it weighs only 62.4 pounds). Movement and placing large stones were easily accomplished by the use of a pry bar and the sheer bulk weight of the barge as a pushing force when needed above.

The external layer of the Great Pyramid was constructed of white tura limestone, which is a different type of material than used in the internal structure. These white blocks of stone were placed in position as the pyramid grew upward. They were effective as an outer seal because of their marble like composition. The polishing of the white covering was accomplished after total completion by lowering the water level in lock slowly as portrayed in illustration 8. At this time of slow water release the external walls of the lock were dissembled also. The polishing removed water marks and discoloration from the outside layer and with the lock disappearing (point A) one of the only traces left of construction method used was the return causeway at the base of the lock. The canal supplying the lock water is also removed. Plate 25 Remnants of well-cut white limestone covering contrast with the roughhewn of internal stones.

Illustration 7.

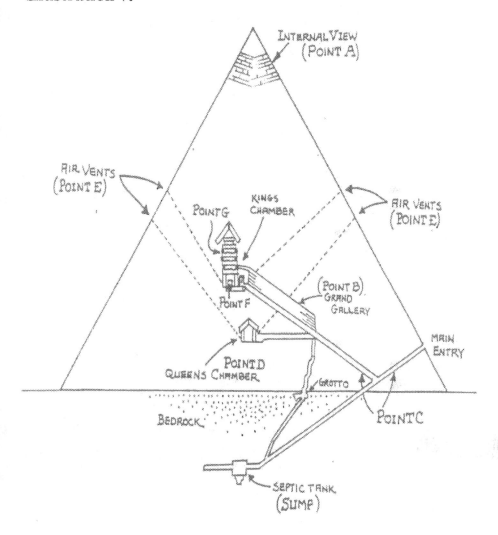

Estimates which have been proven somewhat accurate, place the total construction time of the Pyramid of Gizeh are anywhere between 15 to 30 years. If this is If this is factual some other source of power other than manual labor had to be used.

It has been recorded that the plundering Arabs needed several generations of time to remove the white stone outer layer to the 70% completion of the pyramid. It is not noted however the number of men or months per year expended to achieve this task.

Herodotus (earlier mentioned) stated that the pyramid was constructed only three months out of the year and that a rotating work force of 100,000 men was utilized.

Illustration 8

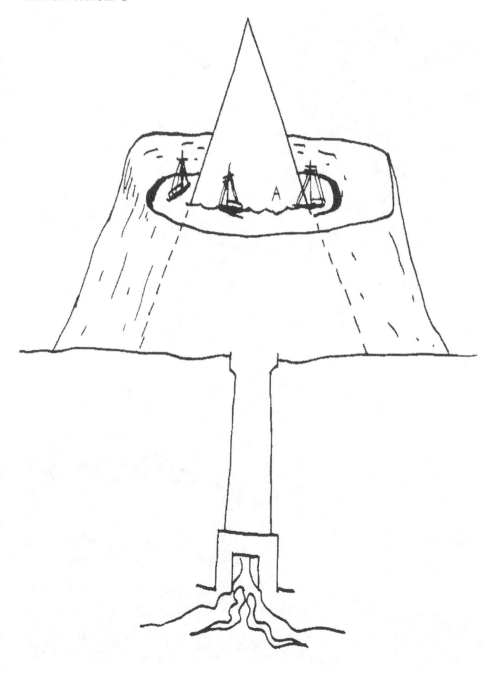

Plate 25

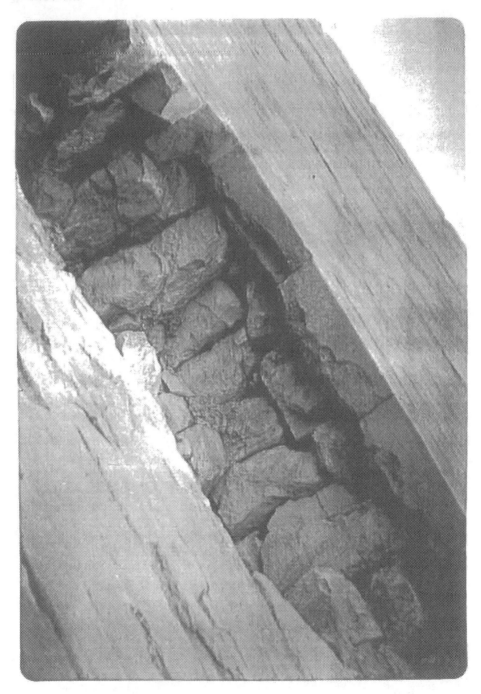

The explanation for this is that the Nile is at its full flood stage for a three month period prior to the date of September 23rd. During this three months flood time no planting or farming is done, producing an immediate work force of many people. These forces of people were conscientious while building the Great Pyramid evidenced by the fact that there is no graffiti written on the stone structure. This feat doubtfully could be accomplished in this day and age even with a smaller work force.

September 23rd is the Autumn Equinox time and it corresponds to the time the Egyptian farmers begin to plant his fields after being released from construction duties. Upon looking at Illustration 9 one can see how the Equinox time was forecast by using pyramid internal sight planes as a guide.

At the time the constellation of Alpha Centaury can be viewed from one side of the pyramid and the Polar Star from exactly the same angle on the opposite side of the structure, the imaginary line that divides the pyramid in half is the Equinox of Autumn. Surely these astrological measuring devices were used in maintaining the proper angle of construction to followed but also, they relate to closely to the flood season to be disregarded as a time measurement device too.

To keep the pyramid on somewhat level plane during erection, spirit levels were used as were reflective devices similar to what the United States Navy uses today (which utilize liquid mercury rather than water) to track the stars and their positions. It has also been noted that the use of pr2 equation during construction was quite prevalent when re-measurement of the pyramid of Gizeh was accomplished. Beneath the Great Pyramid is an angular drain passage as shown in Illustration 9 point A. It is interesting to note that all of the angular passageways in the pyramid are connected to it. At the base of this drain is a large sump Point B with a leach line connected to it Point C. Until now, this was thought to be an underground grotto but upon closer observation, one would have to agree it is an exact duplicate of our modern day septic tank system.

Illustration 9.

EQUINOX

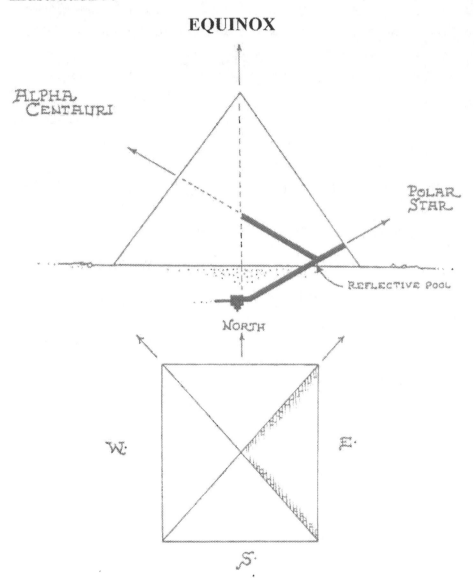

Illustration 10.

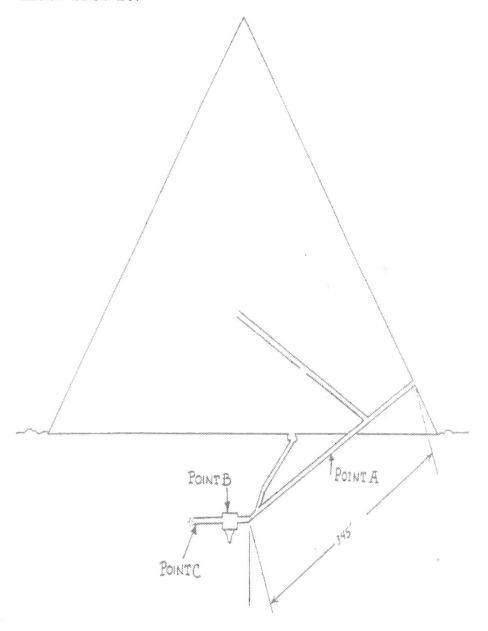

This system was used to clear all water that may have accumulated due to leakage or spillage from the lock itself during the construction process.

CHAPTER VII

ARCHIMEDES

To better understand the "Canal and Lock Theory" and how the massive stones used to construct the Great Pyramid were easily handled, Archimedes Principle of buoyancy and water displacement has to be understood.

To say that the Egyptians "invented" the principle of buoyancy years before Archimedes is probably more than just conjecture. For example, the 70 plus ton gable stones would be much easier to position if their weight were reduced under water and then utilizing the water as a form of lubricant, to allow careful positioning so that the stone would show no scrape or chip marks. Whether or not the Greeks should get credit for many mathematical theorems and solutions or merely recognized as interpreting the Egyptians engineering efforts is an interesting question.

The formula used to calculate the displacement of an object (submerged) is "an immersed body is buoyed up by a force equal to weight of the volume of fluid (water) it displaces".

Everyone has experienced the effects of buoyancy, and how objects in water appear lighter than the same object on dry land. But many may not know the math-ematical formula that describes this effect. Archimedes principle says that the apparent weight of an object in a liquid is reduced by the weight of the amount of liquid that the object displaces. The most common liquid where these effect are realized in water, which has a density of 62.4 pounds per cubic foot. So hypothetically, let's say you have a 70 ton granite rock; the density of which is about171 pounds per cubic foot. Its volume would equal 70 tons X 2000Lbs/tonX171

Lbs per cubic foot = 819 cubic foot. The weight of the displaced water would be 62.4 Lbs/Cubic foot X 819 Cubic foot= 51,088 Lbs. So the weight of the submerged granite rock under water would equal 140,000 Lbs. – 51,088lbs = 88,912lbs; a 37% reduction. Or to put it another way, the weight of a granite object underwater would be about 63% of that same stone's weight on dry land. Another example is a 5 cubic foot stone used in construction of the pyramid would weigh 5 cubic foot X 171lbs/cubic foot = 855lbs on dry land, but fully submerged in water the same stone would weigh 855-(5 X62.4) = 543lbs.

All of the other various sized building stones used in erection of the Great Pyramid could be measured to ascertain their density factor, and then actual amount of weight and manpower required to move the stones could be ascertained.

CHAPTER VIII

THE SUMPS

The one identifying characteristic of pyramids that were completed by the "lock and Canal System of Construction" is the presence of a "sump".

Previously named "Grottos" or "Lower Chambers" by other researchers, they were all designed and built with similar function in mind.

Listed are the first easily recognizable design traits of the sumps:

1. Most are below the ground level of their respective structures.
2. The majority of them are "fed" by and connected to the angular passageways.
3. Their sizes and shapes are of the volume to handle and dissipate large quantities of water.
4. They do not reflect high qualities of workmanship as found in the tombs and aisles located above ground level.
5. Most were constructed of brick, stone blocks and mortar.
6. The base chamber of the majority of these "sumps" has a leach line connection to it. See Illustration 11

There is a practice followed by many researchers of historical and ancient races and their structures. It is to find the "refuse" or trash sites. For some reason this practice has not been followed completely when studying the pyramids.

The underground sump could possibly reveal more about complexities of pyramid construction than can be imagined. When the rush of water filling these sumps, during and after the construction process, flowed downwards through the passageways, it is feasible to think that tools, artifacts, and various waste remnants may have been transported to the bottom of the sump. Surely by checking out the sumps of some 70 plus pyramids something of value could be revealed, but the restrictions placed by the present be revealed, but the restrictions placed by the present government of Egypt prohibits this research. There sumps may have filled in due to collapse of their walls or may have been hidden by other sealed off passageways.

Plate 26. Fresh water shells litter the area around several pyramids. Some have been found on the top of the pyramids indicating either a high point of submersion or extensive flooding of the pyramid's location.

When one looks at pictures of various pyramids, several intriguing points of similarity can be seen. The pyramids of Dashir and Gizeh have entrances that are well above the ground without steps leading to them. Was this because they were surrounded by water and that possibly people were "floated" to the entrance?

When looking at pictures of the Pyramid of Cheops and Meidum there are definite signs of erosion that encircled the complete pyramid much like rings in a bathtub. Were these "erosion rings" caused by allowing the pyramids to stand in various depths of water for great lengths of time (i.e. 20 or 30 years)?

When discussing the "Canal and Lock Theory" and inevitable question always arises. "What happened to the canal walls around the pyramids?" In all probability they were disassembled after the pyramid was completed. The only trace of the canal walls are square shaped outlines which are starkly visible today when viewing aerial photographs of the structures. Plates 27 a,b,c,d,e. "Erosion" levels of construction are indicated by lines around pyramid. These lines are best viewed from a distance. Usually at 30%, 60% and again at 90% levels. However, some of the sand canal walls are still visible around several pyramids that were never completed (i.e. The Meidum Pyramid). The Gizeh complex

Illustration 11.

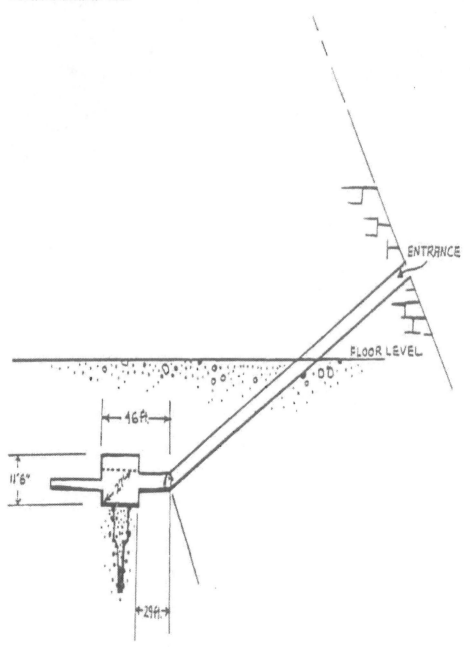

Plate 26

Plate 27 a.

Plate 27 b.

Plate 27 c.

Plate 27 d.

Plate 27 e.

is always referred to as being built on a plateau. But in actuality Gizeh Pyramids were built in a basin which, topographically, may have been much deeper during the pyramid era.

It can also be imagined that 4000 years ago, the Nile River may have been much higher than it is now in relation to the Great Pyramid, as it is a swift running river. For example, the Colorado River located in the states of Utah, Arizona, California and Colorado, carves its course deeper and deeper into the walls of the Grand Canyon in Arizona. The Colorado as it cuts inches wider each year, also alters its surrounding land form.

Natures with its erosive elements have hidden some facts that could support this theory. Still physical existing factors are found presently that do lend support and credibility

One such factor exists twenty miles north of Cairo, where stands the remnants of an earthen "fort". When Flinders Petrie wrote his observation of the fort in the early 1920's, he stated that its walls were 200 feet thick at their base and 40 feet thick at the top. The square area that the fort encompasses is 10 acres. Petrie made an observation that the "fort" was un-Egyptian like, but in the same description he stated that it had a causeway, which is typically Egyptian. The "fort" (Illustration 12) was supposed to have been built by the nomadic tribe during Hyksos reign of Egypt (circa 1350 B.C.) for the purpose of protection and yet there were no structures inside the "fort" to protect according to Petrie. There was no entrance to the structure. Now the "fort" is nothing but rubble, and the causeway that Petrie wrote of does not exist any longer. At this point some supposition is used. Could this "fort" be the remnants of a reservoir built to start a pyramid that was never completed? And, could it be possible that the nomadic tribe merely used the walls as shelter rather than receiving credit for building them? Only more extensive research can produce the answer. One question that raises interest concerning the "fort" is why anyone would build walls 200 feet thick to stop arrows and spears? Only earthen dams and reservoirs have walls constructed so thick. The vast area that is encircled by the "fort" (redundant) is very close to the enclosed area of a reservoir needed to construct the Pyramids of Dashir. To add to the mystery of why the "fort" was constructed one would have to imagine the around of labor expended to build such a structure in the first place and what protected the labor force while the "fort" was being built.

If all the questions asked were answered even if negative to the theory, the results would be interesting highlight of ancient Egypt's history.

Illustration 12.

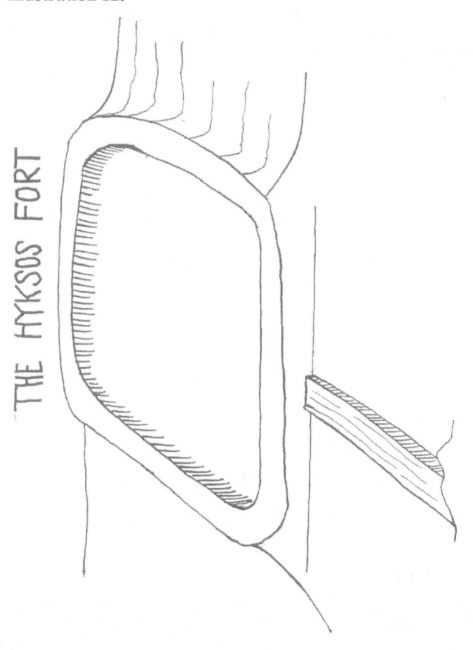

THE HYKSOS FORT

CHAPTER IX

THE STONE HARVEST

E very new theory must be put to the test. Such was the case when the "Canal and Lock Method of Pyramid Construction" theory was developed from its infancy stage five years ago. Proving the theory beyond a shadow of a doubt is impossible at this time. Full cooperation from Egypt and adequate funding must be made available to complete the research needed before the Canal and Lock Method of Pyramid Construction can be made a proven fact.

The last research trip to Egypt it took six weeks of strenuous work on the part of my colleague, Mr. Geoffrey Purcell, who did an excellent job considering the rather low budget afforded him. Even though Mr. Purcell's rather expensive SLR camera and some artifacts were stolen from him toward the end of his stay in Egypt he returned in good spirits and health. The theft was unfortunate for another reason. The photographs of the Hyksos fort were still in the camera that was taken. The majority of the pictures taken and samples from various pyramids were not taken, however, which was a godsend. Lack of cooperation on Egypt's part was somewhat understandable for reasons mentioned in earlier text, but it did hamper the research considerably. The lake of travel and communication facilities in Egypt, which are archaic, did not help matters either. In spite of drawbacks, the results were encouraging. On top of the Great Pyramid, silt deposits were found underneath the exposed internal stones. This silt was indicative of water being at that level of the pyramid for a long period of time as the silt layer thickness was over ¼ of inch. Salt flakes were recovered from the Queen's Chambers in the Great Pyramid. The salt samples were flat in shape and had dirt residue on both sides of the flakes. Recovering the flakes was very difficult as the gallery leading to the Queen's Chamber is a narrow, rubble filled, and fetid smelling shaft. The sale was leached from the stone used in construction and from the water of the Nile. It continues to come out of the stone even today.

The sumps underneath the Pyramids of Gizeh have yet to yield any artifacts or tools. They are in such a sad state or repair that entering them could be hazardous. The closing of Dashir area negated the checking of the sumps in the Red Pyramid. Again if only more cooperation from the Egyptian officials was available, the sumps could have been opened.

When checking for the air shafts holes at the 60% completion level of the Great Pyramid, they could not be found because of the external rubble. Finding them would not have been too consequential because the shafts were filled with debris and animal dropping which would have blocked further research of them. The shafts are still quite important as they are a necessary key to locating internal tombs in the stone pyramids. It is known that air shafts were started from the Queen's Chamber in the Great Pyramid but was not completed (as far as research tells us now). The shafts were completed to the King's Chamber and Gallery. Some important questions arise now. Are there other air shafts in the Great Pyramid? Are there undiscovered shafts in the other stone structures? In all probability, yes. Finding the shafts could lead to a bountiful harvest of history. Within several pyramids, only the sumps and lower chambers have been found. No upper chambers or galleries such as the ones located in the Great Pyramid have been discovered yet.

How can the internal tombs be found if they do in fact exist? By utilizing the Canal and Lock Theory, it is know the exit holes of the air shafts are probably above the 50 to 70% level of construction in the pyramids. It would be a simple process, simple with cooperation from the Egypt to enter various pyramids through existing openings and fill these chambers with heated, colored air. This would be done with smoke generating machines equipped with a heating device. Once the cavities inside the pyramid being studied were filled with heated air, all known exits would have to be sealed completely with plastic cloth. This plan of action sound very amateurish but it must be noted that this is a modification of the method used to locate air shafts in mines and caves. The process works. An infrared camera or a starlight night sighting device has to be used in the middle of the night to detect any escaping hot air. Scanning the pyramid especially at the 50 to 70% level, would probably be best don in the very early morning hours of darkness in order to let the outer walls of the pyramid to cool down. If any seepage of hot air is detected at any point of the aforementioned levels, that would probably be where the air shafts exists and could be located. If the colored smoke was visibly escaping during the daylight hours the same procedure would have to be followed. Once a shaft were located it would be necessary to find out where they lead to inside the pyramid by using probes, lights and cameras. If an internal tomb or gallery could be located it would certainly be exhilarating and fruitful.

Another test and use of theory possibility could be used to locate pyramids that do not exist above ground any longer because of previous dismantling of discomposure. This could be accomplished by studying aerial photographs of both banks up and down the entirety of the Nile River for traces or remnants of ancient causeways and whether or not old cause ways paths lead to square mounds of sand or depressions. It should be remembered that just because a pyramid no longer stands, the ground portion of it could still be intact.

Plate 28. This drawing by J.G. Wilkinson show the square outlines of the reservoir walls that remained in the 19th century. The boat pits were not shown as they were not discovered until later in the 20th century. Note the

Plate 29. An early depiction of an aerial view of the Pyramid of Gizeh drawn by Norden in 1740. Again Norden mentions canal and dikes.

Plate 30. Archeological "dig" site are prevalent throughout Egypt. Although many items of ancient Egypt's past have been unearthed, one can only imagine what is left to be discovered. Plate 31. Remnants of

Plate28.

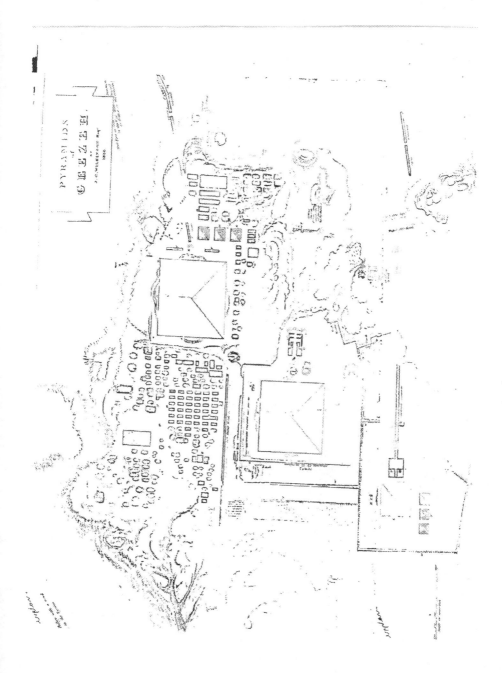

Plate 29.

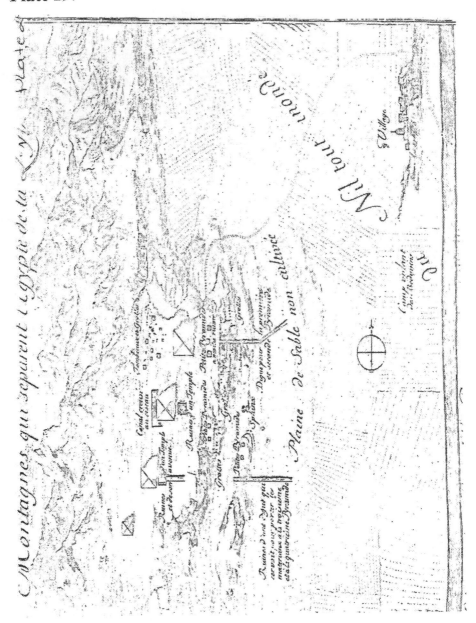

Plate 30.

Plate 31.

Plate 32.

the causeway that lead to the Great Pyramid. The stone blocks used to pave this causeway are of a basaltic nature and are darker in color with the granite blocks used in the pyramid's construction. Plate 32. The walls of this ancient causeway are under reconstruction. According to the "ramp" theory of pyramid construction, the massive stones used were dragged up these passageways. The base stones of this causeway do not reflect much wear, and do not lend support to the "ramp" theory. Plates 33a, b, c, d, e, f. Causeways were long and narrow with thick high walls and well placed base stones. Nearly every stone block pyramid had a causeway leading from it to the Nile River. Most causeways are not in good state of repair. Some are only pathways littered with stone remnants. Plate 34. The size of ancient causeways is well represented when comparing them to the three horsemen in the background.

By using sophisticated metal detectors on the discovered sites, perhaps metal tools or artifacts could be detected to pinpoint an underground structure. This plan of research is severely hampered, as aerial photography is practically forbidden in Egypt, due to the military situations that exist there. One can still hope however that this situation will not continue forever.

In the course of completing this book, a question was asked that took some time to answer. "If the theory is released, why give away the knowledge that might lead to discovering Egyptian Treasure?" Without sounding like a prophet, the inquiry was answered" "Egypt's greatest treasure was knowledge and the ancient Egyptian's application of it." the inquiry was answered "Egypt's greatest treasure was knowledge and the ancient Egyptian's application of it." This treasure can only be discovered and shared with cooperation and respect, not plundering, greed, and distrust.

Plate 33 a.

Plate 33 b.

Plate 33 c.

Plate 33 d.

Plate 33 e.

Plate 33 f.

Plate 34.

BIBLIOGRAPHY

Aldred, G.	Egypt to End of the Old Kingdom, London 1965.
Edward, I.E.S.	The Pyramids of Egypt, Rev. ed. Harmondsworth, 1961 and London, 1972.
Fakhry, A.	The Bent Pyramid, Cairo, 1939. The Pyramids, Chicago, 1969.
Mendelssohn, K.	The Riddle of the Pyramids. United States. Pracger Publishers, 1974
Macaulay, D.	Pyramid. United States. Houghton Mifflin Co.
Petrie, WM.F.	The Pyramids and Temples of Gizeh. London. 1883. Meidum, London, 1892.
Herodotus.	The Histories. Various Editions.
Rawlinson, G.	Herodotus, History of the Greek and Persian War. U.S.A. 1963. Washington Square Press, Inc. New York
Tompkins, P.	Secrets of the Great Pyramid. United States. Harper & Row, Publishers, New York, 1971.
Hewitt, P.G.	Conceptual Physics. A new introduction to your environment, United States, 1971,1974. Little Brown & Co. Boston.
Nat'l Geographic Society	1978 Mysteries of the Ancient World. 1979National Geographic Society, Washington D.C.